the words you're not hearing

the words you're not hearing

illustrations by Olya Patrushina

We go through many different
chapters as we co-create the novel
of our life. Some chapters are light
hearted, full of expansion and
excitement, others are weighed down,
shaped with grief and confusion. I
believe each chapter serves an
important purpose in the make up of
all that we are and have been in
order to help us process the past,
make room for the future, and
everything in between.

My hope is that this book offers a
gentle mirror and loving embrace to
support you in the chapters you may
want to skip over.

IT IS THE SPECTRUM OF EMOTION THAT MAKES BEING HUMAN SO
BEAUTIFUL AND EACH CHAPTER DESERVES TO BE HONORED.

you are
supported.

surrender

this year,

spirit led me on a journey of
answering this question:

what would happen if you let yourself

                              rest?

fully, truly

           R   E   S   T

to not give up on your vision,
but to take a second to just pause the constant effort for a moment
to reflect on how much you just went through and where it brought you
to not gloss over it, as if it wasn't a major life changing experience
to let yourself sit in all of it

the heartbreak
the fear
the doubt
the expansion
the new opportunities
the perspective shifts
the reset
death and birth

my god

what would happen if you just let yourself rest in the melting pot of all of that?

what would happen if you let go of everything you thought you had to be in order to
be worthy,
and allowed yourself to lower the burden of pressure and expectation?

what would happen if you completely changed directions for a bit
and experienced what a different path might have to offer?

what would happen if you let yourself off the DAMN hook already?

If you took a moment
to breathe
and digest
everything you had been through

what would happen if you let go of control for just a minute
and went with the natural flow that was presenting itself to you?

what would happen if you dropped each identity
and let yourself explore what it feels like to be fully expressed?

the wild
the primal
the mistress
the artist
the child

what would happen

if you stopped judging it so much

and gave yourself the chance to

just
not
know

and that be

ok

for a while

rebel

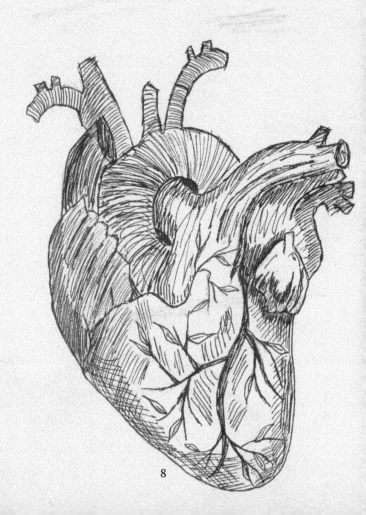

stay open

why do we stifle the heart
when all it wants is to
connect
without restriction

i want to love
because
i love

not for the result of what that love may
...or may not
bring about in another

i can only control my
love
and move from the core
of that...

my love
my heart

walls

what would happen if you dropped your walls down a little bit
if you were vulnerable again
what would happen if you let him into your life, but not your body?
if you let him into your body, but not your life?
what would happen if you took the hinges off and let the animal out?
if you gave permission to the demons inside to run the show for a bit?
what would happen if your darker aspects weren't always being asked to be transmuted,
but instead given the driver's seat
what would happen?
if you realized how much of you was left behind in the name of being
"good"
"successful"
"worthy"

and then you said f**k it to all the rules
so you could go back and discover the incredibly dynamic

S   E   L   F

that lives within you

that's been patiently waiting to be witnessed by you

that's been there all along,
knowing that one day you would make it

Here.

Experiencing.

what would happen

escapism mix

ask me how this past year has been
and ill tell you to look at my top spotify
playlists

it reads
escapism mix

laughed when I saw that
because all too accurate
this year, although it's been about
getting grounded
i've just been trying to find my way out of it
and the thing is,
i've been somewhere squeezed between two
boulders
there's scratches all over my shoulders
bruises up and down my legs
open cuts on my forehead
and dirt under my nails
from trying to create enough distance to pull
my body out of this tight compression
that these boulders have wedged me in

when I set out on this expedition
i couldn't have anticipated the avalanche
that brought me to this predicament

and now—
escapism
how do I get out of this?

the sand in the hourglass is running thin
sun will be going down soon
and I can't hold onto hope much longer that
someone will stumble over
come to my rescue
before its too late
and the wildlife preys on what's left of me

vulnerable to their attack
i can't fight back
ill grow weak from the struggle
get devoured before I can offer rebuttal

escapism
is the only way
but...

between these boulders
i can't find the strategy to get out from
under this weight

never

never
and i mean never
regret being open to share a love
more than surface deep
never apologize
for your soft edges even if
the knife creates a wound that won't stop
bleeding.
never regret being open
not even when the one you gave yourself to
had no space to hold you

never apologize for being one
to give more than you take

these are things
an open heart will go through
you will want to stitch it closed after them
but know this as truth
the world needs more lovers
like you

so never. ever
regret being
open

call me crazy

if the truest aspects of me have desires that you call crazy
than so be it

call me crazy

i'm learning how to let that be music to my ears
instead of it adding fuel to my fears

so tired of watering down my dreams
just because you think that what I want is
out of reach

some. stupid. fantasy.

i used to believe you,

when you would educate me on the reasons why
what i wanted was not ever going to be
but then i found mirrors
reflections of that part of me
in so many other crazy minds around the world
and finally was able to see

that it wasn't me who was crazy
it was you who refused to see
the potential in this life

the wonder, the adventure, the abundance, the beauty

my soul isn't wanting these things that are unattainable
it's wanting me to follow the desires
and remind myself of what is truly capable

if that's crazy
then i'm on a sure-fire path to insanity
and contradictory to what you may think
my mental health just keeps getting better from living life this way
so although i'm tired

so. fucking. tired.
of defending my dreams and
the way my soul speaks
helping hold up societal structures that i'd rather see crumbling
tending to fires of a distorted humanity
when really i'd like to be a part of the team that's putting them out
and bringing forward the waters that can cleanse collective catastrophe
build it all back up with massive capacity to live compassionately

i'm more than ok with being called crazy

go ahead
i've heard it once and i'll hear it again
call me crazy
one day maybe you will understand
when you see where this crazy takes me

rebel

rules
tired of them
who controls them anyway

who's to say
success, this way

puppets
herding sheep

single file
follow, don't lead

pretty sickening
the homogeneity

wake up
this is what they want
refuse to be a pawn

individualism
amiss

humanity
hindering bliss

one thing i know
that is not the way

only rule to listen to

trust what lights you up
let that lead

fuck what they say

rebellious? maybe
but that's the choice i'd make
day after day after day
if it meant i get to be me
along the way

rules
tired of them

gonna play this game my way

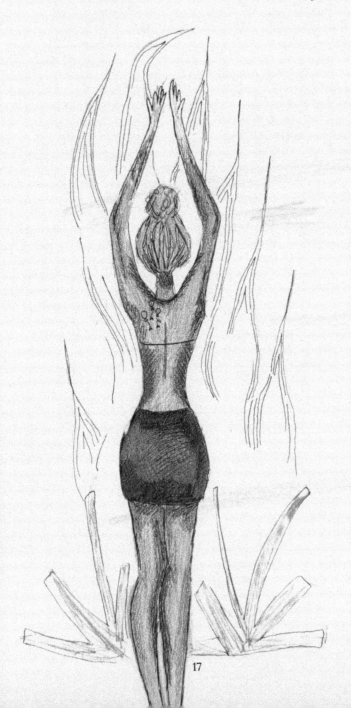

17

self care

start living for you

not by some strategy that tells you
how to get from point a to point b

start living for you
whatever that may mean

maybe you get on stage after a few drinks
kiss that boy in the bathroom
with the neck tattoo and nose ring

maybe you skip through the streets
let your inner child steal the show
howling at the moon
when she comes out to say hello

maybe you take it slow
write songs and poems that naturally flow
as soon as you get still
gravitating closer to that place where you
feel
connected to your soul, less alone
or thrown into the middle of an emotional
landfill

maybe you go off grid
remind yourself what it's like to be in an
experience
without having to document it

frolic in a field
where the flowers and the trees are the
only ones in the know
no witnesses to see you barefoot
free and feral
enjoying that pb&j sandwich
underneath your favorite willow

maybe you wear that bright dress with
the cut-out back
post whatever, whenever
even the less than humble thirst traps

maybe you book a one-way
not just for the classic escapism vacay
but for a whole soul led exploration
deep dive, culture shock
put yourself in a new environment
with very little planned
let the universe create the map
time releasing the clues on where to go
next

whatever it is
do it for you
not for a world that may or may not respond
life is short
we hear this all the time, so
what would you do with your time
if your life was on the line

start living for you
do things that make you admire the hell out of yourself
things that create that kind of abundance
we call inner wealth

start living for you
not for validation and praise
cause what does that even matter
when you get to the end of your days

start living for you
today
what excuse do you have
that justifies to wait

modify

modified
ridiculed
picked apart

to meet some standard
some...bullshit, made up, no ground to stand on
standard
of
what is appropriate
what is acceptable
what is proper

who do you think you are to decide what i choose to stand for?

modified
ridiculed
picked apart

she isn't lady like
why?
because she refuses to follow a rule that says sit like this
wear clothes like that
don't be too much

or too loud
or too proud
or too...
or too
or too
or too.

so let me ask you something
what would be enough for you?
how would you like to modify the way that i look so you feel comfortable?
how would you like to ridicule the way i live my life so that you can feel better?
how would you like to pick apart my looks, my words, my actions, my art
the many different facets of my being
that i'll have you know
make me the me that i've been working so damn hard to be
how dare you stand unwavering with your standards
expecting me to bow down and agree

21

don't you get it?
we've moved beyond that
so excuse me as i refuse to be picked apart
as i refuse to self betray for one more second
to tend to a broken system
that has told me nothing but

> how to be
> how to speak
> how to dress
> how to act

from the very tender start
excuse me as i tear up the rule book whose only intention has been
to dim
this big, strong, lioness fire that is burning in my heart
excuse me as i scoff and hiss and dismiss
the stupid fucking standards that have made me like this
i no longer want to be appropriate
i want to be free
i no longer want to be acceptable
i want to be free
i no longer want to be proper
i want to be free
don't you get it?
you have no control anymore
so go ahead
modify, ridicule, pick apart
but i'll still be here
outside of the box that you put me in
standing for myself
not your standards

misunderstood

i'm learning
that it's ok to be misunderstood
that even those who know me
intimately
may not really
know
me

selfish

here
a raw part of my heart
it's been beaten down
tenderized
marbleized
cooked up
to be served on a plate
only for you to cut through
as you do
devouring it
for your own personal
gain

pillow/lesson

maybe i'm too much for you
i think that's the consensus i've come to
you weren't looking when you saw me
standing in harsh fluorescents, new kid on the block
fragile to touch
could you tell i was still reeling from the shock
no, how could you have known
the way my world had chewed me up and spit me out

a pillow and a lesson all in one
you couldn't see what was coming
and somehow landed right in front of me
i, too, was deceived

see
the only way i knew how to love was unconditionally

a pillow you rested on
a lesson i am still learning from

they tell you to make sure you hold your own
and never let others cross your boundaries

but a boundary is tough to understand
when those in your life before always ran
so you'd give a key to your inner world,
hoping that was the way to stop them from returning home

a boundary is tough to understand
when the reality of what is happening was not written in your plan

a boundary is tough to understand
when what you want is to collapse the distance between
and hold their hand

a boundary is tough to understand
when all you've known is a wall you can never summit

so, ok
maybe i'm too much for you
that's something i've had to accept
but it's not something that makes me want to love less
i wasn't looking when i saw you
and i know that can happen again
i've been trying to loosen my grip
trust the unfolding
surrender
to all of it
and if a boundary is what is needed
i will do my best to find a way to uphold it
i've grown sturdier over time
built some non-negotiables of how i want to be treated in
this life
so a boundary will come more easily
as i've turned the focus on loving myself unconditionally
a boundary will come more easily
when the other side of the coin doesn't seem to be
flipping
a boundary will come more easily
as i take back my power on the life i want to be living
a boundary will come more easily
now that i've been the pillow
and the lesson
there will be less room for second guessing

maybe i'm too much for you
but i won't be for him
or them
and i sure as hell won't succumb
to dimming to half of who i've become
just because
You
feel like it's...
too much

27

type

just know that i'm only going to keep giving you love
because that's where i'm at
i don't mind if that's not your type
this heart i bare craves to be open
expressing care
even when the other party is struggling
to open back and receive the love that is there
it's scary, i know
which is why i've gone through what i have
for the depths that i have
to the extent that i have
up until this point
so i can stand here with you
feel no warmth
yet move from my heart still
risking to be left alone
turned down
battling a current that is on trajectory to kill
but hold strong in love
trusting it to overpower
knowing there's no other way
so
love leads the way
it always will

raw

give me substance
i'm bored, can't you see
it's lost its charm
the same damn story on repeat
isn't there more to explore here?
i can't be the only one aware
this narrative lacks that thing...
the one we are all so desperately seeking

show me what's underneath
what would happen if you gave your inner voice the mic for a change
let your heart speak and soul lead
let me in, in a real way
surpassing skin deep
give me more
or maybe give me less
what does it look like to be a fly on your wall?
when you're not manipulating your stance
and the words expressed are unedited and raw
i'm longing to know that version
give me that angle
not just the same filter you use to hide the things you call flaws
tell me
what do you do in your free time?
what makes you angry? do you get anxious?
are you missing what it felt like in the past?
or feeling conflicted on where to go next?
i'm tired of this shallow way we are connecting

i want to weave between the lines
break through the facade
modify this worn out storyline
i don't care if you think it's too heavy
give me some insight
what hurt you along the way?
did your childhood leave marks that never seemed to fade?
i can see you're afraid
what is it that keeps those walls so high?
i want to know more
like
what happened that first time you gave your heart away?
have you been following your dreams?
what gives you a sense of purpose?
and what is that song
the one that you can't stop singing
let me in
i promise i'll hold onto you with carE

i'm just so sick of not being able to go more than half way
when i know damn well there is more there

too much

oh i'm sorry
was my depth too much for you
did you want just another
pretty silhouette
to fill that void
you refuse to look at
so you keep both eyes wandering
shape shifting in the night
body to body
chasing the next momentary thrill
waking to another on your pillow
yet the warmth of her does nothing
hollow inside
still
addicted to the chase
have you ever felt
what it's like
to be on the other side of
casual, surface, power play
to get close
and not
run away

to be loved
and not
leave
have you ever felt
what it's like
to walk through a door
and actually
stay
to merge your life
and co create with another
to share who you truly are
and stop with the games
have you ever felt
what it's like
sometimes I wonder
was my depth too much for you

rather

i would rather feel the depths of loneliness
than go back to feeling numb and cold
i would rather experience the heaviest heartache
than go back to closed off and apathetic
i would rather touch the edges of the greatest despair
than go back to living life avoiding emotion
i would rather lean into the many layers of my shadows
than to go back to only accessing a limited version of myself
i would rather go through 1000 deaths
than to go back to staying stuck in a restricted box of what life has to offer
i would rather allow the world to see me in the fullness of pain and grief
than to go back to hiding behind a trembling smile
i would rather be cracked wide open, wounds exposed
than go back to walking around as a shell of a human
i would rather breakdown in public
than go back to

one

more

day

of suppressing what i truly feel

twisted

what if i want it to be confusing
the thrill of what move may be made next
when you leave at the same time as me
walk me to the car
and let lust take the reigns

what if that's something i have been missing
and though it hurts like hell
when the next day comes
and i know damn well you won't be there

i still
get excited for the next time
because in some twisted way
that confusion
keeps turning me on
so what if i don't care that there's a barrier
an area of connection that we just can't reach
can i be ok if this is all that lives

between

you   &   me

the silent stares
in a room full of mutual connections
where nobody knows we shared the same pillow and laid under the same sheets
three times this week
and even we can't make sense of what is going on
as we walk this fine line of lovers and friends
what if i want it to be confusing
subconsciously

        it's something i crave

after years of what felt monotonous
lacking fire, passion and desire
that tension that makes me act a little crazy
when you come close for a second and then pull away
so am I tricking myself
i question if i'm losing my balance
reverting back to silly adolescent ways
but i can't deny that maybe i like playing this stupid game
and I like the uncertainty of if you're going to stay
because the rush of that is much more appealing
than a love that was so sure it became
well...
          boring

so go ahead and let them judge
because i can't tell if i'm ready to pull the plug
i might lean into the web you're weaving once more
and hope that i make it out
but for now
i'm intrigued by this wave you have me riding
and what if I want it to be confusing
before i meet the next one who will bring stability
instead of always having one trigger finger ready
before i meet someone who will stay
and give me a reason to open fully
to surrender in his embrace

before that one who will change the game
i can linger here
in your mess
and enjoy the shit out of this pain

the words you're not hearing

blank page

writing keeps me sane

just me and the blank page
it's the only place that i feel safe these days
the only space that won't potentially turn away
so i'll share what i need to share
and i know it'll listen without judgment
it'll hold my anxiety
nourish my need to express
and there's no fear of rebuttal
when my emotions go apeshit as my soul starts to undress
so much energy moving through my body
a literal vibration prying at my pores
like a charge of electricity
as i put these relentless feelings into words
and allow what's in my subconscious to be heard
that might sound absurd
but that's why i turn to this blank page
it never offers me advice
it never tries to calm me down or give me a different perspective
it just holds the space
as i ramble and rant and blurt whatever the hell I want
whatever is on my brain

i'm honestly so tired of these feelings
three years, isn't that enough
of the karmic cycles adding up
don't i deserve a fucking break
some relief at least from these feelings that are so damn hard to shake
some days it feels like i walked down a path that lead to a door i was forced to open
with no clue at all what i was opening it for
and now i'm in this dimension that i can't get out of
but i've hit my max, i'm exhausted, and i'm done exploring
some days i want to go back
have less awareness of the planets and how they transit
be less in tune with the phases of the moon
and less conscious of the wounds of a lineage that i have come to help transmute

some days i crave a blank slate
that's why i come to this blank page

resist

drowning

drowning
how can i feel so centered on this wave
but still be drowning
i swear i'm doing my best
to keep strong and keep calm
shit
i changed my whole life for this
and it's just hard sometimes
to always stay inside the lines
look for meaning and signs
but end up
here
again and again and again
i'd be lying if i said i wasn't fed up of trying
so
damn
hard
for what?
for another lesson
to add onto this karmic web
drips of honey drawing us closer
trying to unwind the knots that were tied before us
but stuck in the mess of it
no getting free from this entanglement
the ancestors have got to be supporting this
i know the world isn't out to get me
but honestly
it's getting hard to see how that can be
because I'm putting in the damn work
to set this lineage free
and the short end of the stick seems to be all i receive

if it weren't for this stubborn faith
i don't know what i'd do
because this journey has given me
way too much to chew

and it's exhausting
far surpassed fatigue
i'm hitting a limit

i'm. hitting. a. limit.

which really is just pushing me towards the
"fuck it" mentality
because what even is reality
what are these structures and confines
that we humans have to live by

it makes no sense
i just wish it made sense

i don't know what i'm doing or where this is all leading
some days it feels like the most powerful opening
while others feel like a brick wall with no exit
just a big block
that's never ending

disassociate

disassociate
defense mechanism at best
numbing agent to suppress

a reprieve

2 seconds to breathe

disassociate

solace
within moments   2 seconds to
too close to open cuts   breathe
salt made its way in

1,2,3,4
the sting   HOLD
1,2,3,4
a feeling too real   RELEASE

gut wrenching   just like that
ear piercing
knees buckling   just til'

too much   the room stops spinning
the room   the knot is untied
spinning   the sound subsides

in recovery from the drop

it's just 2 seconds to breathe

self discipline

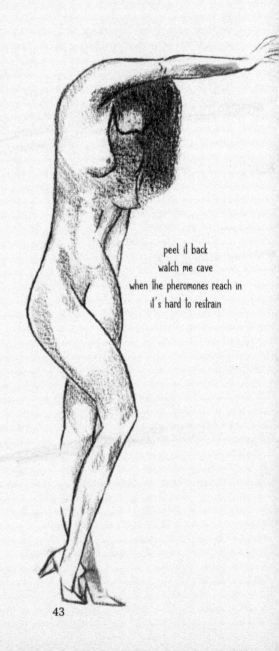

peel it back
watch me cave
when the pheromones reach in
it's hard to restrain

self respect

trying not to be attracted to you is
         like
shutting down a piece of me
that has her hands out begging
and i made a promise
     i
         wouldn't do that again

so i meet with this inner space of
    resisting
cause i know attraction doesn't make up for
the other things that are missing

self destruct

immersing myself in anything besides your memory
has been a class 10 challenge
i'm fighting a battle with my inner demon
and she's winning

i know for my mental health
i should wrap myself in anything but
your memory
it's intoxicating
this heartbreak
what kind of crazy am i
if i say i like this feeling

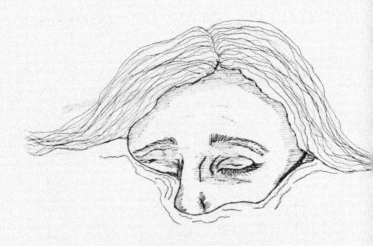

45

your memory

im on a writing spree
i guess that means your memory is invading every thought i think
i guess that means im not over you like i thought i'd be
every hour i write is another obituary
every line carrying a piece of you
the ink bleeds with each word left
like a needle
tatooing your existence onto pages before it too can escape me
still acting as a weak remnant of glue
i guess there's nothing left to figure out
but i still see you every time the sun goes down
and when i wake
and when i drive
and when the clock has a number between 1-5

i see you
i hear you

echoes of a voice that used to be so close
i guess that's something i'm just going to have to let go
something that is a story of the past
doesn't need to be retold
maybe one day you'll let me in again
and then i won't be relying on old pictures to remind me
it will be your heart
where my inspiration will be born

element

something in the simple things

        like the way your clothes fit on your frame

and the way you look when you have nothing to say

see, i have this tendency to latch on to the idea of you
to fantasize while i watch the way you move

i want to see you in your element
so i can see your essence
        without the withholding

allow myself to be mesmerized by what it could mean

if I maybe one day love you

        if I maybe
      one day

        love you

reciprocity

mutual effort
is not too much to ask for

scared to lose you
but i didn't really have a grip
did i?
my fingers kept slipping
so what would i be missing
if i stopped clasping so tight

the true mystery
if i let go
is there enough foundation built
to sustain

am i the one holding this together
a weak container
that if not patched up
will just start leaking
emptying the contents
until there is none

letting it all go
testing the stability
testing out lack of control

what are we really?
been wondering if i'm the only one
feeling anything real

letting it all go
giving it a chance to breathe
a faulty boomerang
cant be so sure it will return

mutual effort
is not too much to ask for
so either this is going to even the score
or it will lead to the next level of closure

questions

crippling questions
space to assume
filling in blanks
what's it like for you?

mental unrest
emotional distress
clarity not there
answers, please share
cognitive dissonance
crippling answer
justification of
radio silence
disconnect
surrender
let go...
wisdom
questions unanswered
solitude initiated
too much space
too much to say
Questions Answers
cemented in place
crippled by
Questions
Answers

busy tone

talking to him because i can't get to you

tried the line
a busy tone is the only thing i'm hearing

you've got the thickest skin
nothing seems to be seeping in

stuck in the passenger seat
of a vehicle that is barely moving

who the hell is steering

patience is a fucking virtue

talking to him because i can't get to you

a lot, too many

i have a lot of love for you

and i'm not sure why
feels like i barely know you
you barely know me
but somehow you're so close to my heart
and it hurts to not be able to to tell you
how i'm feeling inside

i have a lot of love for you

we never let each other in
except superficially
that's all this was
i was just temporarily fooled

i have a lot of love for you

i've written way too many words about you
these thoughts don't seem to quit
they circle around
without a landing pad
my minds been trying to sort through it

so i sit here, allow it all to come out
speak my mind
into the nothingness
the space between us

i have a lot of love for you

warm body

if just for tonight
can you help me feel less alone
i want to lie next to a warm body
lately my bed sheets have been feeling so cold
i know it's a temporary fix
right now i'm ok with
the morning will come soon
i'll try to forget what it feels like to lie next to you
your heart under my hand
my head on your chest
if i can hear the sound of life
maybe i'll feel a little less dead
so if just for tonight
hold me close
i want to feel another's skin
i know it's a temporary fix
right now i'm ok with

look

it's ok if you want to look
i'd rather you see me
naked
than turn away

loyal

plenty of people
to lock eyes with

but i get fixated on

you

took a slice of my dignity

i keep waiting for the day

you

decide to return it to

me

shell

as soon as we go there
you shut down
how could someone with your career
touring the world
stage to stage
not be able to speak these things
not have anything else to say
you just shut down
it's not worth it
not something you want to go through
rather keep it to yourself
all the way until the day you rest

sadness.
but you call it contentment
simple.
the way you want it

at least,
thats what you always say

i wonder what broke you back then

your shell
indestructible.
no matter who tries
a lost cause

rather keep to yourself
all the way until the day you
rest
you like it this way

at least,
thats what you always say

i wonder what broke you back
then

as soon as we go there
you shut down

ceiling fan

badgered by an inner voice
that never ceases
flipping through emotional damage
and all the doors of desires
whose keys i haven't been given

is

a type of hell i can't wait to not be in
i've never believed in a place called heaven
but right now
to get out of here
i'll believe in anything

gaps

why must I read into every detail
details that you don't seem to think about
at least not out loud

is there tension here
or is it just that you're so damn unclear

                    it's not fair
      to leave me grappling with questions
          only you have the answers for

i'm making up stories to close the gaps of
this year

  to end the conversation anytime you decide
              it's time to go
      to always leave me wanting more

the vagueness
leaving blank spaces
space
never seems to evade this

          is there tension here
  or is it just that you're so damn unclear

stuck in your mystery
i can't escape it

             i'm making up stories
        to close the gaps of this year

is there tension here
or is it just that you're so damn unclear

      tired of expecting things to change
     when the details remain the same
    and the situation is set on replay

if you could just look me in the eye
i feel like i'd be able to understand why
or at least weed out the lie

        everything is so damn grey

cant you just tell me why
you always look away
as soon as the moment enters into the grey

         is there tension here
    or is it just that you're so unclear

            i'm making up stories
        to close the gaps of this year

2

we're more alike than you think
2 souls 2 kids 2 homes
watch this

it's all in the lines
left it behind
the days of passing paths
trace of connection hard to come by
nights closing with
2 bodies
lost in translation
relying on the comfort of the sheets

tell me what it means
words create silence
leaning in closer trying to listen

something here i'm missing

tragic
heartbreak leaves imprints
yet, a crime scene with no evidence
2 hearts
pleading the 5th

silence
2 souls 2 kids 2 homes
gone silent

oblivious

we didn't know what we wanted then
why can't i let it go
replaying memories that went wrong
reminiscing on illusions
hoping for moments that will never come

i replay that moment in the kitchen
was there something else to say
that could have helped me convey
all these fucking feelings we don't know
how to name

things are fine now i think
but i still keep spinning on
things i shouldn't be missing
spiraling
cycling through
all of these thoughts about you

what's wrong with me
that has me thinking
things will ever change

a fantasy not worth holding
a blueprint that will never make it to
bold ink

giving you the time you never said you need
and space you didn't ask for

I'm too sensitive to not pick up
on the subtle clues you don't know you make

so tired of this give give give
not even sure you know how much you take

oblivious

you're so oblivious

do you get a thrill out of it

because it just leaves me
writing a bunch of words that you'll never
know i did

59

.your eyes

i never know what you're feeling
so i'm sorry if i trigger you today
your eyes, they tell me more than you do
so don't blame if i don't know what to say

you always come back to me
with that piercing stare
i can't see clear, there's a stupid glare

what am i supposed to say

i can't read your mind
and your body language isn't doing much either this time
i know it's there, hidden in plain sight
but the only thing left to rely on is

your eyes

you'll never know
my body language has learned to dial back too
it's not only you who gets to run
this time
i'll keep you at a distance
cause even after trying to fix this
i still never know what you're feeling

but it's in your eyes
the missing pieces to this story line
the way I know you care
how you try so hard not to cry
the mutual attraction that hasn't gone anywhere
the curiosity of what is left to salvage
if anything is left to salvage
is anything left to salvage?

you always come back to me with
that piercing stare
but nothing to say
so if i walk away just know

you make me uncomfortable
because you feel so comfortable
but none of this is comfortable

i never know what you're feeling
the vague demeanor leads me on
inside i'm screaming

it's in your eyes
where i wander to look for answers
despite the knowing that
i'll never know what you're feeling
it's in your eyes
but i need the words to make sense
of the last 6 months of events
the trust i had in you is dwindling

it's in your eyes
but i need the words
i just need the words

you always come back to me with that piercing
stare
but nothing to say
i can't continue to never know what your
feeling

61

reset

moments

i find myself most in these moments
when i can't get out of my head
and the anxiety has risen to my throat
when i can feel all the cracks in my body being filled with fear
of the next stupid thing i'll say
or the way it will feel when you walk away
the moments when i just want to scream
tell you all the things that never came out right
because my nervous system didn't know how
so instead, i just shut down
but cover it up with some surface response
that was probably 99% nonsense
the moments when i'm scrambling for some semblance of peace
within the crevices of this internal landscape
that feels like it's ripping at the seams
i find myself most in these moments
after i've come to terms with the realization
i was holding on too tight
to a storyline that simply wasn't how it was meant to play out
when i have reached the point
where i turn to
Stillness
Nature
Breath
when I finally let go
in whatever way i can
to stop giving so much meaning to it all
and remember the ever changing essence of this

i find myself most in these moments
because i have to face that
no matter what
i'm the one i need to love most
at the end of the day
and the rest is simply a mirror
i find myself most in these moments
diving past the illusion that voice inside wants me to hear
and making my way to listen
closer, deeper
to the voice that whispers
    "it's all ok, you are safe here"
it's all ok, you are safe here
the voice that reminds me
i can't fuck up anything meant for me
and i can't force anything that is not
the voice that reminds me to let go
to let go to let go
i find myself most in these moments

seam

each thread seems to lead to loose ends
the seams keep fraying
a clean stitch isn't staying
need a new technique to stop this fabric from coming undone
the seam,
why won't it stay?
think there must be something i'm doing wrong

not the best at knitting
i guess i never really gave it a try
so when the thread gets all tangled
can i be surprised?

with this kind of thing
you have to get it right
you can't fake your way
pretend you're good at it
and expect the product to stay
together
it'll just
unravel

loose ends aren't easy to hide

the seam,
why won't it stay?

avoidance

you just keep running away
i guess that's the trend
seems to be pretty popular these days
just two people playing this game
there's the one who runs
and the one who pursues the chase
it's getting boring
this game
can we please change the rules
being able to predict your next move
really kills the mood
it's a part of nature, you know
this cat and mouse thing
but my god, it's so immature
my god, it's so immature
what the fuck is wrong with people
why is honesty too much to handle
why is being vulnerable
such a widespread scandal
and why in the hell
do you keep blowing out this candle
i thought we were on to something
but where were we going again?
i seem to be blanking
maybe there's no such thing
maybe this thing is broken
society...
human relation...
can we try to sort out a new solution to this equation

sparknotes

i feel like you are a test
i'm just trying to make sure i pass
because if i'm being honest with myself
i wasn't always the best student in the past
missed a couple assignments
sometimes skipped class
learned the lesson the hard way
and if I don't want a repeat
i should probably show up this time
pay closer attention
do my homework
everyday
you're giving me information to work with
and it's best if i don't gloss over the details
not gonna lie, i was a fan of Sparknotes
but the knowledge was temporary
and i just have a feeling that's not the best thing
i think you might be my chance for a redo
trying not to fuck it up
it would be stupid of me
to let this opportunity to go to waste
and not study the material
come prepared on test day
i feel like you are a test
i'm just trying to make sure I pass

tuesday.

just wait til tuesday
there will be more information to gain
and it really does no good right now
to rack your brain
over things you have no control on
the conversation cannot be rushed
can only take place organically
on tuesday
if at all
cause we both know
it's been an on going question mark since last fall
so just remember to take it day by day
knowing that this fog will eventually fade
and the light will flicker
until it gets enough energy
to turn back on
to shine
on everything that has been lost in translation or become
a missed opportunity along the way
dont stress yet
tuesday
you will feel it out then
just like you have in the past
you can be confident
you've become prepared
more and more
for
what the universe has in store

landing pad

doing what i can to make you feel comfortable in my presence
but i can't do that anymore without betraying myself
that fixer nature in me needs a revamp
and i'm trying here
to let your soul do what it needs to
so we can maybe grow closer
while giving eachother distance
and i'm fighting the temptation to reach out
to hold your heart with warmth
give you a soft landing pad
because unfortunately
i know that's not good for me
or for you
in the long term
the divine plan has a different blueprint
for what our souls are longing for

magic 8 ball

did the energy shift
are we going back to how it was
round in circles
will we ever realize there's no resolution to this
because i'm shaking this magic 8 ball and I keep getting the same thing
the answer is
not ready yet
ask again another day
pulling any semblance of meaning
every marble in one basket
and one basket only
fate
i'm just really tired of playing this game
this giving giving giving
but not being reciprocated

loving me when it's convenient for you is not enough

nothing left

has it been long enough
is there nothing left here
i want to ask you
but i'm afraid

tell me i'm wrong
that there's nothing left here
and i'll leave it alone
finally give myself the chance to move on
give you what you've probably been
wanting all along

without the question
of if i stay
would you admit it to yourself one day

and would we start over
from the spark that never went out
would there be enough oxygen
to sustain something so fragile

am i delusional
is there nothing left here
has it fizzled out

been burned to the ground
to start anew wouldn't do any good
nothing left to tend to in the fire
it's run out of tinder and wood

i guess i just want you to see me
even that would be enough
know that we got the chance
to undress for a moment
to stop covering up

i guess i just want you to see me
maybe that would be enough

72

friends

months
that's how long it has been
since you and i could be considered friends
but don't twist my words
that doesn't mean i'm not happy for you
moving on, starting over, being better
i want that for you
but i want just play it cool
i've learned my lessons
tightening my boundaries
building stronger filters for what i let in
so, no
we're not friends
we're not cool
we're far from
that space between us just grew
and grew and grew
and now I don't even feel like I know you
everything you do makes me feel shitty
so i am trying to stand my ground here
i don't want to fall back into my pattern of quieting this scream inside so you can't
hear
i want to make it known
that whatever friendship we had, what it could've been
its lost now, its over
because you decided to let go

so, no
we're not friends
we're not cool
we're far from
that space between us just grew
and grew and grew
and now I don't even feel like I know you

broken nails

when i need to check my mental state
i look down at my hands and it's a
reminder
torn cuticles
brittle, thin
broken skin
exposing a pinkish red
puffiness

so when i need to check my mental state
i look down at my hands
but remember to do so with grace

time spent in the back hallways of my
head
shown in the self destruction of my nail
beds

because life is a bitch

and sometimes you fall behind
it's hard to be in a race with anxiety
when it's skilled at compromising competition
and is always the first one to break through
the tape
at the end of the race

i'm not sure why i continue to do this
well aware of the consequences

hot sauce and rubber bands and sitting on
my hands

nothing can compete with the speed of
anxiety
it will always win the race

the urge to quit is so strong
but sometimes an addict can't resist the
high
and when the lows hit
there's not a comparable vice that will stop
the temptation of giving in

3am thrill

open but afraid
bracing for that moment
the sting hits and the high fades
like that lake effect chill
on a Buffalo winter day
piercing
the tension, paralyzing
and simultaneously liberating
you don't look the same
memories of you start to make me wonder
was it you the whole time
or some spell you had me under
illusions always get me
things have shifted
puzzle pieces rearranged
dry erase markers made this story
temporary, kinda blurry
leaving slight traces of what was
what used to be
you know the story
but don't get me wrong
i'm in no hurry
what is is satisfying
gratifying
a new page to fill
new morning eyes and 3am thrill
new city, new hand to hold

and i'm ok here
it feels still
in the peace of this now
not tied to any string
nothing holding me down
flying solo, levitating above the clouds
no need to come searching
not like there's some lost and found
so watch that distant light make its way
from orange to yellow and yellow to gray
watch the image of me take flight
light to dark, dark to light
it's all the same anyway
and honestly
there's really nothing left to say
i'll save the rest
for another day

butterfly

once again,
she doesn't feel like me anymore

my own company

browsing through my thoughts for inspiration
scanning all the items in this location
conversations back and forth
in my mind
really anything to pass the time
think i'm running out of things to do here although I love speaking with the sun & wind
and i've learned to be content with the stillness found within
only so much of that i can do until I wonder if i'm losing it
and losing grip
getting lost in the 5th dimension
lost in the mystery
lost in the cosmic joke of what the hell actually is
reality
hearing the laughter from the trees
as they watch me try to figure out what I could possibly do
to occupy myself in a way that might be a little new
minute by minute, the day just stays in place
and i just keep staring into space
ok, i admit, i feel... insane
i love spending time with myself, don't get me wrong
gotten used to all the feelings that i get when i'm alone
and even when i'm lonely, i can still be happy
but, man i'm pretty bored of my own company
maybe i could find somewhere to go
grab a seat at a bar
put my headphones in
act like I do that often
people-watch and tune into others stories
pretend for a minute that they're talking to me
god, do I sound crazy?

i´m pretty bored of my own company

do you do this too

it can´t just be me

mental recess

i turn music on
when
my thoughts get
too loud

only so much
i can write down

when i listen more
i can think less

a mental recess

seen

when I feel like no one sees me,

music does

sting

it stings less now
but the rip of that bandaid
left my skin burning
pain reverberating
the fade was slow
and each time i made a move it seemed like running through a field of thorns
a rose garden with threats around each corner
and an open sore that never has time to heal

leaving me with words for days to describe how that sting feels
but never words to tell you
because that would make it too real, right?
you couldn't handle taking responsibility

too much time passes

so i'm left trying to remember us through old photographs
and a time capsule that reads

a life that would never last

low quality bar

can we go back to before
when i had no desire to
hold your hand
no understanding of
what it felt like for you
to caress my skin
                back to before
when the idea was
not even a seed
things were easy
my mind was free
                back to before
you said a lot of shit
you didn't mean
and got me questioning
what the potential of this
could maybe be
                back to before

simple
a low quality beer
in a low quality bar
random groups
loud music
dark rooms
before any romance
deep talks of
not readys
and miscommunication
making the foundation unsteady
can we go back to before
drop it off all there
the moments
the memories
the words

the words that never
went anywhere
let's drop those off too
leave them for dead
for good
to be devoured like prey
to return to the earth
put them to rest

for now and for always

82

games

playing hard to get here
it's your turn to chase
we can keep this going
but this time i'll be the unavailable one
let you know i'm not interested
then at night, end up in your arms
learned that from you
it's fun right? i'll act like i don't care
like i don't notice the distance you are creating
but make sure to keep that fire burning
quietly tending to the wood
i know eventually you'll come back
wanting to receive the warming
the soft touch of my lips on your skin
but no more looking at the rules
it's better to play with chaos
so let's go
i'm all in
scramble up the pieces
shuffle the cards
roll the dice

let the games begin again

reset

patience

throwing a fishing line into a lifeless sea
watching for the water to bubble
to move the bait into place
where there would be
reason to anticipate a tug
why do i keep trying
this receiver seems to be broken
wishful thinking
hopeless romantic kinda dreaming
to sit at a payphone waiting
for you to ring in

proximity

proximity
- room   for questioning
this.
it's fleeting, right?
a memory
momentarily passing
not to be - everlasting
add it to the list
things to reminisce
when the weight of night
coats the room
your energy lingers
but   you.
nowhere in sight
just moments
just memories
from a time
proximity
was on our side
been looking for
something to
stick.
solidify.
fossilize.
it's ok to take - space
let the lights dim
the colors fade
sometimes
within the grey
is where you find
clarity.

fleeting

fleeting
it's all
fleeting
poems
roll off
tongues
lullabies
only stay for
the night
feelings
left in the
memory
a blip in
time
fleeting
hands waving
a signal for
goodbye
nothing promised to
last
enjoy it now
in a moment
that moment will
pass
fleeting
nothing promised to
last

dead end

how do you spend your days

      the minutes and hours that no one sees

in the moments of

          mundane

what gets to know you in that way

i wish i didn't know what i do

          tender knowledge

ii didn't come from you

open room

      to guess the validity of my source

what words are actually yours

thought there was more road to cover

but this path   is a dead end

unfortunately for me

        i care about you in ways that don't make sense

so i've been putting up with it

    the half assed messages   sorry attempt to be friends .

but truthfully

i hope i've had enough
      i hope i've met the point of exhaustion

because i deserve so much more
than to be a second
      or third option

i thought at the very least   you would meet me in the middle

Instead

you get off in remaining
      an unsolved riddle

damn poetry

i always fall for the damn poetry
gullible to
sweet sound of manipulation
rolling off the midnight flickering of the stars
catching the iris between innocent mischief and intentional deceit

it just doesn't make sense to me

                                why say things you don't mean

i'm not in the mood to let it slide
this time I'll say what's on my mind

i'll tell you that I started to care
until you proved you didn't have the courage to be there
showed me that it was an illusion
some sick twisted delusion
a way you like to use to your benefit

get what you want then just...

                                 get rid of it

i knew it from the moment you said you liked me
before you even knew me
so how could you like me
you just liked the idea
guess I wasn't what you thought I would be

guess the illusion was prettier than the real thing

but fuck if I'll apologize
for just being

89

fuck if I'll apologize
if you cant find rest in that bed you made

fuck if I'll apologize
if my words get a little heated

you made this mess
so idk what story you've been hearing
sorry not sorry
i'm not just a body

not just somebody you use
at your convenience
when you need a dose of sympathy
as a temporary fix when the truth you're harboring hits

and you reach for that dopamine slick to replace the heaviness
that is stretching its arms out
inside the hollow cave taking up all the square footage in your chest

done giving more than i'm receiving
that,
my cue for leaving

told you my fears from the beginning
that's where i went wrong
cause you used them against me
funny
i thought you'd be different
but jokes on...   you

you missed out on a girl that could have shown you something beyond the surface
shit you've been perpetuating
guess that's something you'll learn in another way
through another pretty face
 another hollow cave

so go and repeat the pattern you obviously feel safe in
speak your lies to someone who wants to listen
cause honestly, I don't care how petty it is
i've got my fingers in my ears
humming to drown out the sweet sound

they say actions speak louder then words
and damn,
isn't that wisdom

so here
let me show you what they mean
as i walk away from whatever illusion we were creating
let me show you i won't put up with it anymore
as I walk my ass out that door
let me show you what words won't
as the silence of the room starts to enclose

i hope you feel it
the words you're not hearing

i hope you feel it

– the words you're not hearing

s i began to trust.

revive

stillness speaks

there are times where i struggle to be still
i guess i haven't learned yet
how to feel content with what is
without giving in to free will
the obsession gets the best of me
in moments between
the space that can't be filled
there's nothing here
new notifications i search for
but why, what for
except to break the silence
the distance
the tension
the longing
why
all it is
all i am
right here
stillness speaks

a phrase that stuck with me
picked it up from this book i read last week
stillness speaks
so why does it feel so damn quiet?
i don't even hear the voice i used to on the days my heart was broken open
in the name of love and devotion
there was a voice...
it took over when the weight of nothingness came through
like a blanket of smoke from a wildfire
it took over when my head was spinning
like a dreidel that hadn't slowed down enough to land
it took over
a voice that carried me when there wasn't a hand to hold
or the comfort of another shoulder
there was a voice
i found solace in
where is that voice now?
why isn't this stillness saying anything aloud?
why is the volume turned all the way down?

if stillness speaks
i'm begging you to turn up the sound
maybe it's my hearing that is at a loss now
if stillness speaks
i'm begging you to turn up the sound

the words you're not hearing

truth

if i can get past the fear of what i'll see

it is in this stillness, that i find true peace

unknown

suffocated by the density of unknown
passion play
like throwing spaghetti on a wall
clarity held hostage
questions without answers
trusting the process...the only leverage

presence

red dot on the map
"you are here"
the excruciating reminder
which will it be? where will it lead?
moving in no clear direction at full speed
slow down

alignment is all that matters
time to review everything, lean in close
make sure you're listening
each day, something new
prior versions don't exist
sifting through the fragments and fractures
identities that have gone amiss
feeling through darkness
gazing through squinted eyes
searching for even the smallest glimmer of
light

unknown, the new home base

presence,

patience

"you are here"

In the unknown
it may not make sense
but

you are safe

here, now, today

constant
these visions are
constant
keep redirecting
focus
focus on the
here, now, today
magnets must be in place
the push and pull isn't
giving way
i haven't found a way
to not get sucked back in
by the electromagnetic
wave
waves keep coming in
never pulling away
no moment to breathe
need a referee
someone call for a time out
everything has been turned
up
when will it go back down

gravity

your law seems absent
how can that be
where the fuck is the
gravity

they say sleep on it
you'll feel different in the
morning
it's been more nights than i
can count
do you have another strategy
that one is lost on me
feeling lost in any company
self soothing used to work
all my senses are set too
high

too alert
too close
too far
too hurt
too much
too loud

for the love of god
turn it down
these visions need
space
time to settle into place

dear one,
it's not that your intuition
is astray
just come here
meet it at this pace

here, now, today

inspiration

inspired by you

when things are in harmony
i'm invited to tap in
let you awaken aspects
i have yet to come to know
the presence
intoxicating
no need to do anything   now
not asking for much   as the turbulence subsides
i'm here

Its an aura thing   Awake, Alive, Inspired
again

so please stay
i want to dive in   something about your soul
please stay   and mine
i feel awake again   a chemical reaction
running through the dimensions
when you left   igniting wisdom
a scorpion stinger sent venom
Into my bloodstream   certain its from another life time
everything went dim
life force weakened   this is not brand new
systems shut down

this
paralyzed   is not brand new

i got lost in the shock of it   whatever bond is present
inspired by it

inspired by you

bad guy

you aren't the bad guy here

but god damn
why does it feel like every move you make
places me in the position of feeling like the victim
out of control of the situation
the one you put me in

how come i have to clean up your mess all the time
tracked mud into my house
left footprints on the carpet
i keep scrubbing
the stain isn't budging

what will it take
is there anything else to lose
do i need to move
    again

how many miles is enough
what age will be an adequate amount of
grown
up

fuck

you aren't the bad guy here
but for once
could you try a little harder to be
  the hero

breadcrumbs

all the breadcrumbs
lead to a trail that is cold and dry and bare
they weren't intentionally placed there

it's better to accept that as truth

operate from the way of thinking that
the way you think about me is not the same as the way i think about you
and since i know what i deserve

which is far more than
actions that don't match words

i'm going to stop giving you the benefit of the doubt
and instead, start rebuilding the wall
in order to keep the distant illusion out

out of sight and mind

it's better this way so i can stabilize my insides

astral

you and i met on the astral plane last night
swimming with speed and grace
in the underworld of the ocean
i'm not sure what we were doing
necessarily
but i do have a strong memory that you were
right there
with me
beside me
somewhere similar to Atlantis

i tried to remember it when i was waking
but all i could see was you, me,
and the journey that had decided to take
through the cities and the communities
it was almost like we were the ones who
governed the whole sea
almost like we were the king and the queen
i know there still a wave we are both riding
just doing it without actually physically colliding
there's plenty of space here now
something i wanted for a long time
and it's interesting to see the themes that still
you and me
are navigating in the same timing
i guess our life together
here
on this earth
has found a resolution
but in the astral
we must be still partnering in some kind of
collective evolution

our souls will never disconnect
and that is something i feel
content with
it's ok if we don't stay in touch in
the way of human and proximity
define for us
because in the other realms it's
clear
we still have something
beyond the human
that is between us

107

muse

so i'll just start writing
because what else is there to do
it's the only thing that makes sense
and it reminds me of
you

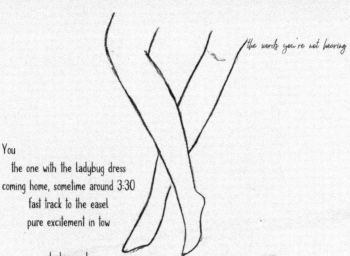

You
   the one with the ladybug dress
coming home, sometime around 3:30
      fast track to the easel
      pure excitement in tow

      splashing color
  so intentional and confident
     peaceful in solitude
  a jar full of creative juice

You

     who indulged in
     breakfast treats
     ankles crossed
     humming softly
  a melody that only you knew
    only you had access to

                      dancing without pressure to perform

You

    who danced and spun
    without a care
  following the inner flow
  from one flail of an arm   just
    to standing on tip toe
    bending and rolling   You

         and how you wanted to play with
           whatever feeling was there

You
      barefoot and blissful
   running through the neighborhood

      exploring the world of imagination
   when you picked up the toys and the dolls
         each new storyline offering
   adventure and travel to places beyond

You
   the mermaid at the bottom of the pool
            sipping tea
            doing flips
   making sure your tail-fin didn't split

         the quiet and gentle
         the sweet and playful
         the little artist coloring
            outside the lines

                              so i'll just start writing
                                 and when i do
                                 i'm doing it for

                                 You,

                                 my muse

reminders

spend some 1:1 time with the sun, and the sound of the birds

you can never know the full picture through a fragmented frame
pay attention to the way you idealize or criticize another

let things run their course
part with them compassionately and honor their visit

intention is everything
it's not about what you're doing
it's about how you're doing it

allow yourself to change. allow others to change
you're not the same as you used to be and neither are they
meet you and them as new, often

give yourself grace for whatever tough thing you're moving through
and when it's time...
let the past be the past

trust yourself more
you know you better than anyone else

sometimes you need more structure
sometimes you need more flow
it shifts depending on your individual needs
let it shift

not everything will have closure
learn to have acceptance for that

not everyone is going to like
                        or vibe with
                                or understand
you

that's ok, there will be plenty that do

have fun with life

you are here to create,
to play,
to love,
to grow

daily love letter

can you love life a little more today

can you welcome it in when your voice cracks
where you want to share but hold back

can you hug tighter
before the release
let the receiving end feel how rejuvenating
simple touch and presence can be

can you pause before returning to a task
that has added up on the list
but you know undoubtedly you will get done
whatever is being asked

can you take a breath
or maybe 2
inhale making space
exhale settling the tension
more and more and more
until the rope that was tired
unravels to its last thread
and the resistance is freed

can you feel it in your core
the connection from above and below
the line that makes it's way from your head to
your toes
and beyond even further
passing through layers of crust
finding it's pathway to the center
of earth, of gaia, of soul, of heart

can you let it in just a little more
stretch the lungs to open up the
pockets in the heart

can you feel the tingle
a slight hum between your brows
something we have access to if we
allow the attention to be sent without
distraction

expand
awaken
arrive

so much love,
life

113

?

sometimes i wonder what would happen if we met again in this energy
have our frequencies shifted
would we magnetically move toward or away
that feeling that i had
the one that i've been struggling to part ways with
would it still be there?
would it even have the ability to exist
or has the field been wiped clean
would my energy and yours be in resonance
or would we find ourselves somewhere, distant, clashing
what would happen if we met in this energy
would you see me the same
maybe there'd be a reignition of that flame
the one that initially drew you my way
maybe there would be nothing left to say
it would feel complete
like what was before was only meant for a past life
sometimes i wonder
although it's not adding up
and there's static coming from the signal from one of us to the other
what would it take to tune in
to clear, open, strong, easy listening

timing

the timing feels off
but somewhere beyond
where we can exist without the confines
of linear structures
or the hands of time
this feels right
like i've known you before
except you were different
and i was too
souls of the same
just contained by different frames
lifetimes of memories
woven through dna
signaling on a level unseen
that i know you and you know me
but that was then and this is now
a moment where those hands have a hold
and no matter what came before
in this life, there's no story to be told
no forcing of something that can't sustain
no pushing puzzle pieces into place
we will let it go
releasing karma
healing trauma

free up the tie that maybe once took its
toll
we will let it go
re-emerge on the other side
knowing that encounter was not meant for
this time
but it was destined for our souls

115

dear god, or whatever

i'ts frustrating to want to share so much
but not know where to do so

dear god,
can you hear me?

is it even "god" that is listening

i mean

who should this letter be addressed to?
i need to make sure this message goes through

so

to whom it may concern
maybe that's the better way to reach you

i have some concerns
and some questions I need answers to

i know there is something at work
my life feels like one project after another
i'm just asking for clarity
so I don't "fumble the ball"
and watch another one of them crumble

dear god,
or whoever...whatever...you are

can you send me a sign?

116

i feel a little greedy,
but i can't help it

this whole being human thing has resulted
in codependence
i feel uncomfortable and needy

and shit, I just need your help
to make it all disappear

so please
please

dear you,
can you even hear me?

let me know you're there
are you listening?

i'm starting to wonder
my connections seem to lack the thing
that makes them
last
and so I'm unsure

life has been a wild time
and I'm just desiring a little bit of
recognition

is that what's happening here too?

when I tune into my body
i know
it's clear

a fleeting call
the slight gust of wind can interfere and
pull under

but quickly
without warning
it all just
disappears

i'm just trying to figure out

is my message getting through?

and left there on the page
words that are reminders...
reason to fear

how can i know?
when i don't even know who i am speaking
to?

reality

has anything i've said gotten through
rambling on this page trying to get to you
keep on making mistakes that i can't undo

has anything i've said gotten through
you're staring into space like you always do
am i speaking a different language
or are you just not amused

has anything i've said gotten through
because it feels like i'm just talking to the moon
airing my dirty laundry
in these lines of poetry
and

i just hope you get this letter soon

ghost

if i could write you a letter
i'd tell you that it doesn't make sense
the way i feel about you wasn't ever grounded in
something real
it was all an illusion
i would tell you how you broke my heart
but it's not like there was much love there from the
start
just you, me, too confused to know what we were doing
or what any of it would mean
i would tell you that it still makes me sad and bitter
and what makes it worse is that every time i see you
the cut that was starting to heal
gets rubbed up against and then i
have to start over
it's not fair
that's what i would tell you
it's not fair that i've been carrying this alone
because you don't seem to be feeling any extra weight weighing
down, chipping away at the density of your bones
nope, you seem to be just fine
another day where i'm not something to cross your mind
you seem just fine
but here
i'm writing this letter that you'll never read
isn't that fucked up?

don't you see
the twisted, imbalanced, dynamic that honestly
you were the one initiating from the beginning
you
you started this whole thing
i was doing just fine
i was finding my footing on the way to a nice fresh lilypad
and now, it feels more like a balance beam
i keep putting my foot one inch too far
to the left or the right
falling, resetting, falling resetting
back to the beginning we go

so i'm writing this letter because these thoughts of mine
they get so tangled and wadded up
and you can't be bothered to be a sounding board
so i'll write down pages and pages of unheard words
i know it won't ever catch the attention of your eye
that's not the point

so i'm writing this letter because these thoughts of mine
they get so tangled and wadded up
and you can't be bothered to be a sounding board
so i'll write down pages and pages of unheard words
i know it won't ever catch the attention of your eye
that's not the point

i'll write this letter
for Me
for my peace of mind
you don't actually deserve to to receive this side
it's too much for you, you've made that very clear
it's too much for you to take notice of anything that
causes you
to be the one to feel
i know it may not be intentional
you're probably blissfully unaware
but i have this new rule
and it's to not justify shitty actions just because someone else has
a trauma response to something
i have wiped the dust off of and revealed
it's not fucking fair
for me to be the one to be left out in the cold
just because you think your emotions for me
are too much to hold
it's not fucking fair
i'm hurting too ya know
except
you don't
you'll move on with your life
and I will too
and that's why i'm writing this letter
to no one
just the illusion of you.

.your head

when you write, what are you thinking about
when you say i miss you
who is it on your mind
who are you thinking about this time
who is your muse
the current project you're pouring into
so damn vague
your favorite game to play
c'mon take a guess
which mask will be the one to show face today
it would be bold
to say i don't wonder
i do
what crosses through
when you see the bed i made
and who i'm sleeping next to
i need to learn an instrument
so i can write songs about this
clear my head
and vent
my soul grows weary
when the thoughts linger too long

so much easier to breathe
making room for them to find a seat
within the lyrics of a song
when I write, it gives my mind an out
a container to release the wild
a place for the angst to feel comfort
as it screams its pain aloud
when i write,
i know what i'm thinking about
when you write
what are you thinking about?

bullet

it's hard not to wonder what life would've been like
dodged a bullet just doesn't apply
i wanted to create a home with you
somewhere along the way
we just lost the light
i thought we could make it through anything
our love was stronger than the rest
but i guess my mom was right
it didn't fit anymore
i was bitter and you weren't in the fight
there is no doubt you showed me love
i forgive you
i forgive me
we did the best we could
and put this to rest peacefully
so i want you to know
i'll never forget the time
you traveled 30 hours to come see me without blinking an eye
or when you showed up in Nashville to surprise me at dinner
and managed to keep it a secret the whole time
or when you set up my yoga mat and oils for when i got home after having a rough
night
picking flowers in the morning, making breakfast, than waking me up with the sweetest
look in your eyes
i'll never forget
because it taught me true love
you set my standards high
now i know how to be treated right
it's hard not to wonder what life would've been like
dodged a bullet just doesn't apply

123

connection

give me a space to share the things that make me tick
provide the opportunity for me to be seen
open up a platform to express my mind
dive into my heart
and experience connection to the divine
it's pretty incredible what happens
in connection that allows for this
the fullness of self
coming alive through the comfort to be
ugly, messy, wild
unapologetically free
a complex multi-dimensional being
is a beautiful thing
when assumptions are erased and restrictions die off
when you find yourself in the playground of life
the womb of creation
in a dance of ever evolving conversation
one topic grows like a weed
branching off in multiple directions
unable to be contained
multiplying at rapid speed

hours of space and time covered
the words continue to give way to a new inspiration
finding yourself coming out of a portal
unsure of where you started, but lit up
by the discovery that has been uncovered
through the joy of simply exploring your mind
in the presence of another
barriers between soul to soul
dissolving over time
meeting face to face with a sense of curiosity
leaving room for the other to be renewed day by day
offering their constant transformation
to not only be acknowledged
but welcomed in
it's pretty incredible what happens
in connection that allows for this

revert

i don't want to go back to my old ways
worrying about slipping into my old phase
worrying about the one i wake up to on a
cold day
or a warm day
or everyday
i don't want to go back to my old ways
it'll just be there with the salt to shake
in a cold way
if i put this to rest
6 feet under
forever laid down
forever erased
maybe then the move forward
will actually move me forward
and these footsteps in the pavement in front
of me
won't be re-traced
i don't want to go back to my old ways
i've come too damn far for that
for the temporary taste of medicine
to be the thing that sends me back
i've come too damn far for that
laying sand where the cement once was
maybe when the wind blows
it'll take away the memories
make space to replace them with something
new

and i can stop going back to the old
ways
recycling this old phase
at some point the material is worn down
and just needs to be thrown away

nothing left to use here
nothing left to use here

repeating that in my head
so i don't repeat anything else instead

i don't want to go back to my old ways

126

aries

your impulsive fire overpowered mine
your confident nature shadowed above me

been finding this year that i actually have
those traits living inside too
just wasn't able to see them
the mirror was fogged by you

your drive made me think i didn't have
what it takes
your protection somehow diminished the
strength
within
the vision i was creating

the mirror you held
the light reflection was too much
blinded me from what was in front
staring back the whole time

this is not to blame
it's because of you i was nurtured through
the alchemy
of a weed to a rose in full bloom

and now
you may not be close but i think you know

it's because of your fire
despite how much was burned on the path

it was you
who grabbed my hand when my toes were
sinking in quick sand
it was you
who gave my tears a container to land in

that i am who i am

your energy, no longer something i'm fighting
to match

i'm holding my own

the flame is coming from the wick of my
individual match

to feel

i wanted to feel free
so i was shown the shackles around my limbs
i wanted to feel independent
so i was shown where i wasn't supporting myself
i wanted to feel stable
so i was shown the spaces my foundation was unsturdy
i wanted to feel pleasure
so i was shown where i was limiting my turn on
i wanted to feel connected
so i was shown where i had lost touch
i wanted to feel fulfilled
so i was shown everything that was empty
i wanted to feel alive
so i was shown where I was dying
i wanted to feel passion
so i was shown where i had grown cold
i wanted to feel peace
so i was shown where i was at war
i wanted to feel
so i was shown where i was numb

teeth

biting down
my cheek, sharp teeth

repeatedly

flesh heals
for a day

then comes the next bite

opened
inflamed

again

my cheek, sharp teeth
meet half way

the flesh
will heal one day

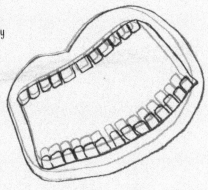

insatiable

insatiable
a hunger born of...
is it
fear, lust, rage
feeding off the flesh
and bones of yesterday
empty plate
after empty plate
what will it take to
satiate

death

the fresh slate comes with so many layered experiences
as does death, yeah?
grief in indescribable amounts
but also the reverence and honor for what or who has died
it's sacred, it's intense, it's tender, it's beautiful
and nature shows us over and over again that the death of something is
not the end.
such as with seasons
each year we witness a death phase, but we always know the life will come again
so how can we not see that within the other places of life?
how can we dismiss that this is the way of nature?
and we are nature
and with that knowledge
how can we even question that our death cycles will not bring new life?

longing

longing
a tug so deep
it feels like
a form of
grief
pain, but
over what?
something that has no name
no face

still
this unwavering desire
a hunger
soul awaiting that thing
to feed and satisfy
the ravenous craving

a balloon

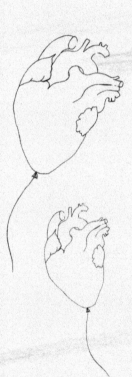

what's it like
to be loved by you
actually
with no strings attached

a balloon
untethered
drifting with the way of the wind

flowing
floating

what's it like

a mystery
a surface yet to be scratched

revive

wishful thinking

how do i stop myself from expecting last year's version to resurface

                            is it...
wishful thinking
                    romanticism
                        or healthy optimism
taking the lead here

don't want to get wrapped up in illusion
that lives within desires
with no end

what will come with smooth waters in the resolution

a calm comfort
soft gaze
love that only waxes, not wanes
will it forever feel unclear
will it ever again feel real
moved past the flames
tired of the sting
the residual burning
karma is on my side this time
haven't i earned that much
after all the brush
waving out and in
the next opening has to be
lush
is that wishful thinking
or is there some truth to this expectation
the outcome i'm anticipating

you are
protected

return

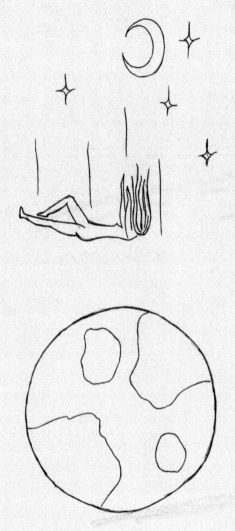

solo

loneliness feels
          different than solitude

solitude is a
          loneliness that you choose

the secret

the secret is that there's no rush
nowhere to be
no schedule to follow meticulously
the secret is that we've been fed this lie
that we must follow a straight line
accept that fate isn't real
and there's no such thing as destiny

the secret is that you can't mess it up
you can't get it wrong
and you'll never get it done

the secret is that this journey is not some linear model
and the greatest growth comes in the times of greatest struggle
the secret is that the human race is playing a losing game
that it's a load of bs when we are told
you can only be successful if you do life "this" way

the secret is to own your own path
and listen to your intuition closely
period. the end.
this is your life to live

2 steps forward and one step back
is a bunch of ludacris
nonsense made up in our heads

the secret is that this journey is not some linear model

the secret is that the human race is playing a losing game

for what it's worth

for what it's worth,
i just want you to be happy

i want you to feel seen by your close circle
and to know that you radiate a hue of indigo purple
i want you to feel safe in the arms that hold you
i want you to trust that support is there when you lose your footing
and that the antidote will be ready to ease the sting
i want you to create from the depths of your soul
and to know that there's admiration for every ounce of your being
i want you to feel secure
to know that your voice will be heard
and to never question your worth
i want you to feel proud of how far you've come
to honor the way you've bounced back from
long nights when the waves of grief left you feeling undone
i want you to scream when you're angry
and cry when you're sad
and to never ever hold any of your big emotions back
i want you to be afraid and do it anyway
to know that you are more than enough
and to shine your light even when the world seems grey

i want you to know a sun that heals and a moon that guides
i want you to be in touch with both your earth and star sides

i want you to feel ease
i want you to find peace

for what it's worth,
i just want you to be happy

reparent

caring for you got me in trouble with my inner child

she knows better and asks me to consult her before i dive in the deep end

my heart doesn't know how to listen to rules

inner child

she's been trying to get through to you
screaming at a blank wall
it's transparent on her end
she sees through
but it is not the same for you
banging her fists up against the edge
trying to get you to notice
but you can't hear a thing
radio silence
to her, you are crystal clear
but to you, she's...nothing
not in the breadth of your focus
out of sight out of mind
she wants to connect
but you don't even know she exists
she wonders if there's a purpose
if her cries will ever catch your attention
if someday the barriers will drop
and you'll finally see
and receive
the messages she's been sending
she's been trying to get through to you
but sound cannot be heard if
there's no one to listen

the best thing

how can i be mad at you
when you're the best thing that ever happened to me
i'm the one who initiated separation
it's not your fault i didn't anticipate the anxiety
or how it would all play out
when you started living your life without me
my puzzle pieces scattered
felt like yours stayed in tact
but i'm realizing i was wrong to assume that
how can i be mat at you
you have a right to change directions
just like i do
and of course the world will feel different
when it's not centered
around a vision that held an image of
me and you
the truth is i'm nothing but happy
and proud of everything we have been through
how can i be mat at you when
you still remain to hold me with care
like my heart is made of fine china
not sure how i got so lucky
to experience that level of care
so how can i be mad at you
when no matter how hard it gets
you're still always there

fortress

talking to you brought light to the fortress that i've built ever since november of 21

vulnerable was always easy to do
with a safe space to melt
and strong arms that held

but since november 21

i've been learning to reconsider
who to disclose myself to
and who is a fire hazard

an obstacle that will cause a blockage
when i'm trying to get through

so, my fortress has grown cozy
there's dedicated room for my vulnerable side to hide
there's shelves of journals with various memories i can't wait to tell
and frames with pictures that bring me feelings of pain and joy and remorse and
i've just learned
when it's time to show and tell
or when it's better to take rest

within this sanctuary shell

unicorn

they say you are rare

and i know that it's true

but i don't want to believe it because what if that means

i'll never find someone else who

treats me the way you used to

the same

you always saw me in a light i couldn't see myself in
helped me feel less broken
showed me what unconditional love really is

i hope i did the same for you

never made me feel disposable
held me on a pedestal
even when my flaws were front and center
you gave me strength to keep the walls from caving in

i hope i did the same for you

you didn't give up when things got tough
my heart could rest when it felt your touch
you reassured me that i was enough
even in my darkest moments
you didn't run

i hope i did the same for you

be here now

i'm learning that right here is ok
and it always has been

that we do not have to constantly strive to be more
those days are over
we have outgrown that narrative

right here

in the confusion we wade through
in the imperfection we can't avoid
in the evolution
and the in between

it's not about dimming the desire to expand

it's about not waiting to reach a version of self more than

this

in order to be seen
and safe
and worthy
and loved

right here is ok
and it always has been

cold coffee

happiness is

a light beam in the sky
prisms created in the glare
a delicate glide of a bird flying by
glistening reflections
bouncing off the ripples from the lake
gentle reminders
stillness between whispers from the wind
a cold coffee in hand
delightful bitterness
sweetness from the rosebush
a brisk breeze on
bare shoulders
little joys on a spring day
basking in the mundane
soft inhale of the open air
sunlight full of giving without hesitation
physical senses activated from earth to sky
energy through the midline
center and ground
simple, calm
presence in each sound
the chirps and hums and buzzing
an ecosystem spanning from roots to stars
working in tandem
baring witness to it all

happiness is
a light beam in the sky
a cold coffee in hand

149

ps.

this life is so beautiful
have you given yourself the chance to feel
that again
or maybe for the first time

So you are given tasks forward to progress on
the infrastructure
In order to someday see the completion
of a project you involuntarily decided to be
the lead on

i know it can get tough when you get
caught up in the blueprint
that traces out each karma with fine line
details with all of the lessons that will be
traversed
as you move from point a to point d
on a journey that you didn't realize you
had signed up for
and at the bottom, in the small print, read

just for a moment
take a deep breath
and look around
put the instruction manual down
take a much needed rest
and....look

*" you will forget everything thing you know right now,
it will be difficult, but one day
you will understand it all again.
ps. you've got this. i promise and... i'm sorry "*

do you see that?

the way the sunlight glistens off of the lake
creating a sparkle as the ripples come and go
like the waves
take notes from the squirrels playing
running from tree branch to tree branch
seemingly playing a game of chase

do you hear that?
listen as the little bird on your front porch
sings a soft tune to you

just for a moment
take a deep breath and look around

shelter

come in, please
lay down, make yourself comfy
i'll nurse that open wound
get you a blanket
a glass of the finest vintage cab
turn on the fire for a minute
here, step out of the cold damp rain
warm up in this sanctuary i've built
i'll share my remedies for your pain
come on in
let me nestle your head in my arms
create the safe space for your worries to fade
let you experience how true love feels
so you don't forget
wait, let me ease that tension in your neck
rub out the knots you've accumulated
throughout the journey that brought you here

phases

let you have your phases
the waxing and the waning
and the avoidance and the complaining
and pushing the button
for self destruction

it's a phase

you'll return after this fades

forgive

forgive yourself
forgive yourself for
every mistake you think you've made
every argument that spiraled
every time you disappointed someone
every time you disappointed yourself

forgive yourself for
all the nights you chose external
gratification over internal progress
every day you spent focusing on the dark
spots of your life
every moment you told yourself you
weren't worthy
or you weren't able
 or you weren't good enough

forgive yourself for
all the pain you allowed
all the times you realized just a little too
late
the times you shut your heart off
the times when you didn't lead with love
first

forgive yourself for
feeling hurt
and broken
and lost
and less than
forgive yourself for
the promises you broke to yourself
and to others
that extra glass of wine you said you
wouldn't have
that bowl of ice cream you felt guilty
about
forgive yourself for
the years you spent stuck in a self
destructive cycle
that trip you never took
that goal you never reached
forgive yourself for
things you did
and
things you didn't do
(yet)

return

forgive yourself
and forgive others

because
        you deserve peace

transform

each limb you sever returns with new form
a path to explore and a path to mourn
we need not tread lightly
instead, it's time to
make a scene
be a trailblazer
create and destroy
and do so unapologetically
let it go, let it all go
then come back
to rediscover with a new lens
allow the collapse of what was
and be present with the new limb
this is the pain and the joy of being human
never knowing all
but always knowing more than we think
it all resides in trusting the instinct

beckoning

the beckoning
you feel it, we know you do
a tug on the rope connected to what you experience as truth
the purest voice you have heard
a signal clear as day
it's right there
the path, the answer, the destination
the way
but then
 - comes again
the swat of a wrist
subtle but mighty -
"snap out of it"
overwhelmed by what is
the many moving parts that haven't found the place in which they
fit
- the practical matters
- the reality checks
- the logistics
and the voice that you were so sure of
starts to once again
fade
but something you will learn is that...
a vibrant soul doesn't easily gray

my dear,
        dear vibrant soul

please, do not give yourself away
the critics will always have something to say
 hold strong
 hold steady
    your light
 we need it
 we are ready

there isn't a better time
It is now we sent the call
It is now your vibrance has something to resolve
It is now, it is now
answer
we've got so much to share with you
answer, dear one
do not withdraw

we understand the risk feels
too heavy to bare
but that voice you can't keep fighting
It comes with support
just waiting to meet you there

157

you feel alone
we promise you, you are not
a whole army is behind you
you will hear us when you slow down the noise
the external judge
the cyclical thought

you will hear us
you already do

it's in those moments of what you experience as truth
those moments when the signal is clear
and you know exactly what to do
it's in those moments
you hear us
you hear - you
vibrant soul
keep listening

you know what to do

the beckoning
you feel it, we know you do

spectrum

i see that symbol everywhere now
not sure how it wasn't something i knew before

spectrum of emotions

        kinda like my favorite thing

to honor and express and make space for others to live within

i'll pour a cup of tea
dim the lights
set up a playlist of sound frequencies

really,
i just want you to know the feeling
of

        true. emotional. safety.

this world has a way of threatening feelings that don't fit into a clean and cut category

but thats not the way it works

we are made up of layers and dimensions
that when given permission to

be

help us learn how to go through life

feeling

through the sunlight and the dirt

welcoming

moments that leave us glistening

being

able to sit with the ones that hurt

fluidity
letting the waves come and go
letting the water rush through
cleansing and alchemizing
the paths that have been trekked by the many renditions of our soul
karma is a part of it
if you don't know your lessons yet
you can be sure that life will find a way to bring you there
but the thing is, it's not something to fear
we all have histories that we can make peace with
if we just allowed ourselves to actually
feel
your days will take you through a range
one minute you may be in awe, the belief in miracles alive
the next may hit like a gut punch leading you to a pocket of past pain
making you question everything about life
this is natural
my god, can we all start to understand
this is natural
can we normalize the
spectrum of emotions
without asking for it to change before it's had time to know it is safe
we are complex creatures
we don't need to always be programmed to the same feature
to fraction off the parts of you is to
lessen the essence
that brings life to experience
more than the conditioning that
offers little room to explore

be easy

be easy on yourself as you cross this threshold from where you are to where you're going
be easy on your heart as it heals from the many times it's been broken
be easy on your mind as it races 1000 miles an hour
be easy on your soul as it regains and builds this new found power
be easy on your body as it catches up to all of its capabilities
be easy on yourself as you find a new sense of peace and tranquility

be easy on yourself
dear one, for you are only human
be easy on yourself,
it's ok to be here, be now, be you

be easy

free will

sometimes the path of surrender
leads to unexpected change

some of which can feel like punishment
aggressive wake up calls
and redirects you weren't ready for

this is where your triggers come online
and trust asks for even more attention

this is where innovation and creation come to the forefront
and belief asks for your hand

where your comfort zone has been stripped
and you are invited to either...
gather your shields and armor for battle
or to enter the field with open arms
ready for the expansion within the discomfort

life calls you forward
but it cannot make that decision for you
that is the job of free will

so when you choose to surrender
make sure you also choose to follow through

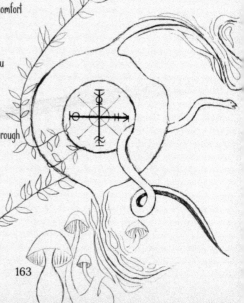

keep going

i know it's hard to believe
but someday you will miss these moments
the times of uncertainty
the destruction of a vision
the early stages of a project
the process of finding your footing again
you will look back and feel reminiscent
of your tender heart
the days you struggled
the inner demons you were fighting
the nights that kept you up
you will feel deep admiration
for the person you are right now
at this very second
in all of your mess
and the ways you keep going
you'll miss these moments
because there is something so sweet and sacred about
the journey of growth
the journey of emotion

this, and

do things you hate, but...
do things you love more
do things that challenge you, but
do things that inspire you more
do things that make you uncomfortable, but
do things that offer you security more
do things that mold you, but
do things that soften you more
do things that improve you, but
do things that feel natural to you more
do things that offer growth, but
do things that offer love more
do things that hurt, but
do things that feel good more

do things for others, but

do things
   for you
       more

octopus tree

do you ever just take a moment

to notice how beautiful life is

when is the last time you stopped to simply appreciate the beauty around you

the nature that surrounds you in each breath

the colors and vibrancy that activates your senses

the contrast that calls you to experience full pleasure

have you forgotten that this creation is full of magical and miraculous energies

have you forgotten that you are one with this energy

what could shift if you just took a minute each day to bask in the beauty of life

166

simplicity

what is the silver lining
she asks me

do you see that tree over there
swaying softly
and the clouds above
shapeshifting

what can you learn from them
what messages do you hear?

the silver lining
it's right there

thank you

I have so many people and moments to give
thanks for in the journey of this project.

Thank you to my incredible support system,
I could not have gotten through the
experiences that inspired this poetry nor
the process to bringing this book to life
without each of you.

To the Pen2Pubnlish writing community
created and nurtured by Allie Michelle,
and to Jordyn Denning for being such a
generous editor. Thank you for your
continued guidance.

To my incredible illustrator,
Olya Patrushina, thank you for doing this
with me and being such a massive part of
what made this book what it is.

To my close circle and the people I love,
thank you for always being there for me
and encouraging me a long the way.

and to each of YOU who is reading these
words, who has resonated with anything i
have written,and who found this book in
one way or another...

Forever grateful.

Thank you for being here

STAY OPEN, BB

about the author

Samantha is an author, holistic wellness advocate, life and energy coach, and yoga enthusiast. She is a spiritual being having a human experience and figuring it out as she goes just like everyone else in this world. Through her work and her words, she shares the depths of her experiences in order to provide a safe space for others that resonate.

Samantha's inspiration to write poetry came to fruition in a personal season of deep shedding and transformation. She likes to say that writing acts as a "comfort blanket" and is honored to be able to offer a sense of peace and connection to others through sharing her poetry.

You are not alone

FEEL FREE TO FOLLOW ALONG

INSTAGRAM - @STAYOPENBB
SUBSTACK - SAMANTHACLAIRE.SUBSTACK.COM/

Milton Keynes UK
Ingram Content Group UK Ltd.
UKHW050159100524
442457UK00006B/33